Living *Water*

a creative resource for the Liturgy

Prayer of the Faithful
YEAR C

Susan Sayers

with Father Andrew Moore

Kevin Mayhew

First published in 2000 by
KEVIN MAYHEW LTD
Buxhall
Stowmarket
Suffolk IP14 3BW

Prayer of the Faithful is extracted from
Living Water – Complete Resource Book

0 1 2 3 4 5 6 7 8 9

ISBN 1 84003 553 6
Catalogue No 1500355

Cover photograph courtesy of
Images Colour Library Limited, London
Cover design by Jaquetta Sergeant
Edited by Katherine Laidler
Typesetting by Louise Selfe
Printed and bound in Great Britain

FOREWORD

A praying church is a living organism, powered by the love of God, and directed by his will. The aim of those leading intercessions in public worship is to provide a suitable climate for prayer, both for the faithful core of praying members, and also for those who drift in as visitors, sometimes willingly and sometimes rather grudgingly.

Since our God is in a far better position to know the needs of each muddle of people who arrive on any particular Sunday, it is obviously sensible to prepare for leading the intercessions by praying for those who will be there, asking our God to lead us with his agenda in mind, rather than taking immediate charge ourselves. Then we have to give him a chance to answer! You may find that a quiet walk enables you to do this, or a time wandering round the empty church, or time spent on some of the mechanical jobs at home while you still your heart and resist the temptation to badger God with good ideas.

The ideas provided reflect the day's readings, and as you read through them you may well find that these ideas will spark off other thoughts of your own. Do use them however you wish – exactly as they stand, adapted to suit specific needs, or simply as a starting point. They are a resource to help you, not a cage to keep your own ideas out.

During the service be alert to what is being said and how God is moving among you, so that you can pick up on these threads, if it seems appropriate, during the intercessions. And if you have young children present, give some thought to how they can also be praying at this time. They might be following a picture prayer trail, singing a quiet worship song, drawing some situation they are praying for, or looking through the intercession pictures provided in children's communion books.

I have heard it said that since God can hear the prayers, it doesn't really matter if the congregation can't. I don't agree. In public worship it can be very distracting to be straining to hear, or isolating if you can hear only a vague mumble. Do take the trouble to practise speaking clearly and fairly slowly in the church, so that everyone can comfortably take in what you are saying. Bear in mind that nerves usually make us speed up somewhat, so speak extra slowly to allow for this.

Finally, don't recite what you have written, but pray it. Pray it both through the intentions and through the silences. Leading the intercessions carries a great responsibility, but it is also a great privilege.

SUSAN SAYERS
with Father Andrew Moore

CONTENTS

FEASTS OF THE LORD

ORDINARY TIME

SPECIAL FEASTS

First Sunday of Advent

*The gathered hopes of generations remind us to get ourselves ready,
so that Christ's return will be a day of excitement and great joy.*

Celebrant
As we think about the fulfilment of all things today,
let us speak with the God of our making.

Reader
We pray that we will all be ready
to meet God face to face,
whenever and however that will be.

Silence

Lord, show us how to live:
and give us the courage to go forward.

We pray that all who lead and advise
may be led and advised by the Spirit,
so that our decisions are in line
with the Father's compassionate will.

Silence

Lord, show us how to live:
and give us the courage to go forward.

We pray that our families and neighbours
may be brought into contact
with the one true, living God
and know his affection for them.

Silence

Lord, show us how to live:
and give us the courage to go forward.

We ask that, through our prayers and our actions,
those hurt by injustice may know support,
the frail, encouragement,
and the timid, reassurance.

Silence

Lord, show us how to live:
and give us the courage to go forward.

We pray that those moving into eternity
through the gate of death
may be welcomed,
and their grieving loved ones comforted.

Silence

Lord, show us how to live:
and give us the courage to go forward.

As we prepare to celebrate Christmas,
let us join our prayers with those of Mary:
Hail, Mary . . .

In the silence of God's stillness
we name any we know
who specially need our prayer.

Silence

Celebrant
Father, you came to show us the true way to life.
Help us progress along that way in your strength.
Through Jesus Christ, our Lord.
Amen.

SECOND SUNDAY OF ADVENT

It had been prophesied that there would be a messenger to prepare the way for the coming of the Messiah. Now John the Baptist appears with his urgent message of repentance.

Celebrant
We know that God is here with us,
and hears what is in our thoughts and in our hearts.

Reader
So we pray for all who claim to be Christians
all over the world.
We ask for a real longing for God in our lives;
a longing that is not satisfied by anything else.

Silence

Holy God:
we want to know you better.

We pray for the different countries
and those with power and influence.
We pray for honesty, justice and integrity.

Silence

Holy God:
we want to know you better.

We pray for those we love
and those we find it hard to relate to.
We pray for a deeper, and a loving forgiveness.

Silence

Holy God:
we want to know you better.

We pray for those in pain
and those imprisoned by addiction.
We pray for healing, wholeness and freedom.

Silence

Holy God:
we want to know you better.

We pray for those who have died
and now see God face to face.
We pray for those who miss them here.

Silence

Holy God:
we want to know you better.

Mindful of Mary's quiet
and prayerful acceptance of God's will,
we join our prayers with hers:
Hail, Mary . . .

As we get ready for the coming of his Son,
let us bring to God our Father
our own particular concerns.

Silence

Celebrant
Father, accept these prayers:
as you prepared humanity
for your coming in Bethlehem,
prepare us to receive you in our hearts.
We ask this through Christ our Lord.
Amen.

THIRD SUNDAY OF ADVENT

*Our period of preparation shifts from repentance
and forgiveness to the freed exhilaration of hope, as the momentous
truth of God's immanence begins to dawn on us.*

Celebrant
God is here with us now.
Let us pray.

Reader
We want to be ready to receive the Lord.
May he take us as we are and cultivate in us
a heart that longs for and worships the God of love
above and beyond everything else.

Silence

Come, O come:
Emmanuel, God with us.

We open to the Father's love
the spiritual journeys of all who walk the way of Christ;
may they be protected from evil
and kept steadfast in faith.

Silence

Come, O come:
Emmanuel, God with us.

We pray for those who give us support,
and encourage us and listen to us,
and make us laugh and share our sorrows.
May their lives be blessed and filled with joy.

Silence

Come, O come:
Emmanuel, God with us.

We remember in God's presence
those whose memories are painful,

and those whose bitter resentment
cramps and distorts present relationships.
We ask for the healing only God can give.

Silence

Come, O come:
Emmanuel, God with us.

We call to mind those we know who have died,
and any who are close to death at the moment.
As they meet the one true God
may their hearts be opened to receive his love,
mercy and forgiveness.

Silence

Come, O come:
Emmanuel, God with us.

We make our prayer with Mary,
who mothered the Son of God:
Hail, Mary . . .

As the love of God our Father fills our hearts,
we pray for any needs
known to us personally.

Silence

Celebrant
Father, we ask these things
through Jesus Christ our Lord.
Amen.

FOURTH SUNDAY OF ADVENT

When we co-operate with God amazing things happen.

Celebrant
As we share in Mary and Elizabeth's joy
at the coming of our Saviour,
let us quieten and still ourselves
in the presence of God.

Reader
We can only marvel at the way
the heavenly Father is happy to work with us.
We want him to know
that we are willing to be used.

Silence

Let it be to me:
according to your will.

We call to mind those
whom we would love to know the Lord
and we ask that their hearts may be prepared
to recognise him.

Silence

Let it be to me:
according to your will.

We pray for reassurance and encouragement
in this parish,
and for insight to the real needs
and what the Lord would have us do.

Silence

Let it be to me:
according to your will.

We ask for the courage
to continue working with and for the Lord,
even during the dark and dangerous times.

Silence

Let it be to me:
according to your will.

We call to mind those who are struggling
with poverty, illness or despair;
may the Lord comfort them,
and use us however he wants.

Silence

Let it be to me:
according to your will.

We remember those who have died
and give thanks for the good
that the Lord has worked in their lives.
May we, with them, share in the life
that lasts for ever.

Silence

Let it be to me:
according to your will.

With Mary, the bearer of God's Son,
we make our prayer:
Hail, Mary . . .

We pray to our loving Father,
in silence,
for everything we need.

Silence

Celebrant
In thankfulness we ask you, Father,
to hear our prayers,
through Christ our Lord.
Amen.

CHRISTMAS DAY

*Emmanuel – 'God with us' – is born at Bethlehem
into the human family. Now we will be able to understand,
in human terms, what God is really like.*

Celebrant
As we celebrate God's coming to us
as a human child,
we bring the needs of our world
before the God we can trust.

Reader
We pray for all those who worship God
in every country of our world.
We pray for the grace
to know and love God more deeply.

Silence

Emmanuel, God with us:
we welcome you!

We pray for those who are spending this Christmas
apart from those they love.
We pray for those whose celebrations
are tempered with sorrow or fear.

Silence

Emmanuel, God with us:
we welcome you!

We pray for peace in the Holy Land
and for all who now live in the city of Bethlehem.

Silence

Emmanuel, God with us:
we welcome you!

We pray for those working over Christmas,
for all women giving birth

and all babies being born today.
We pray for their homes and families.

Silence

Emmanuel, God with us:
we welcome you!

We pray for those being born into eternal life
through the gate of death,
and commend them to God's love and mercy.

Silence

Emmanuel, God with us:
we welcome you!

We join our prayers with those of Mary,
who shared her joy with the shepherds:
Hail, Mary . . .

We pray in silence, now,
for our own particular needs and concerns.

Silence

Celebrant
Heavenly Father, accept these prayers
and give us the strength and the will
to walk in love,
through Jesus Christ.
Amen.

First Sunday of Christmas: The Holy Family

*Jesus' perception and understanding of his purpose and work begins
to take shape throughout his childhood in the Holy Family.*

Celebrant
We have been called
to pray for one another in God's presence.
Let us settle ourselves to do that now.

Reader
We pray for all who are called to lead and teach
so that the truth of God's love
is shared throughout the world.
We ask for wisdom, energy
and sensitivity to God's prompting.

Silence

Incarnate God:
we love you and we need you.

We pray for all with power
and influence in our world.
We ask for a widespread desire
for those qualities of compassion and integrity.

Silence

Incarnate God:
we love you and we need you.

We pray for all parents and their children,
especially where there are conflicts,
anxious moments and gaps in communication.

Silence

Incarnate God:
we love you and we need you.

We pray for all missing persons and their families,
all who are rethinking their direction,
all who find life full of contradictions
at the moment.

Silence

Incarnate God:
we love you and we need you.

We pray for those who have come to the end
of their earthly life,
especially any who are unprepared.

Silence

Incarnate God:
we love you and we need you.

We make our prayer with Mary,
Mother of the Church:
Hail, Mary . . .

As members of Christ's family,
we name those we know
who are in any particular need.

Silence

Celebrant
Father, we ask you to hear our prayers,
through Christ our Lord.
Amen.

SECOND SUNDAY OF CHRISTMAS

Christ is the way God tells people about himself.

Celebrant
We have met here
in the real presence of our God.
Let us pray to him now.

Reader
We bring to mind the worldwide Christian Church,
both leaders and people,
as we begin another year.
We ask for a deeper awareness
of God's presence among us.

Silence

Though we cannot see you:
your love surrounds us.

We bring to mind the troubled areas of our world
where corruption, injustice and violence
ruin lives and damage self-worth.
We ask for a renewal of heart and a cleansing grace.

Silence

Though we cannot see you:
your love surrounds us.

We call to mind those we have spent time with
over this Christmas season;
we ask for a blessing upon all our families,
friends and neighbours.

Silence

Though we cannot see you:
your love surrounds us.

We bring to mind all who live away from home,
all refugees and all children in care.
We ask for the security that only the Lord can give.

Silence

Though we cannot see you:
your love surrounds us.

We bring to mind those who have died recently
and all who grieve for them.
We ask for comfort to be given to the dying
and the assurance of the Spirit's presence.

Silence

Though we cannot see you:
your love surrounds us.

We pray with Mary,
who so tenderly nurtured her holy Child:
Hail, Mary . . .

Now, in the space of silence,
we bring to God our Father
our private petitions.

Silence

Celebrant
Heavenly Father,
we ask this through Christ our Lord.
Amen.

THE EPIPHANY OF THE LORD

Jesus, the hope of the nations, is shown to the world.

Celebrant
We are all companions on a spiritual journey.
As we travel together, we pray to God our Father.

Reader
We pray that the worldwide Church
may always be ready
to travel in the Lord's way
and in his direction.

Silence

Light of the world:
shine in our darkness.

We pray for the nations
as they live through conflicts
and struggle with identity.
We long for all peoples
to acknowledge the true and living God.

Silence

Light of the world:
shine in our darkness.

We pray for the families and the streets we represent,
asking for a spirit of generous love,
understanding and mutual respect.

Silence

Light of the world:
shine in our darkness.

We pray for all who are finding their way
tedious, lonely or frightening at the moment;
for those who have lost their way
and do not know what to do for the best.

Silence

Light of the world:
shine in our darkness.

We pray for those who have come
to the end of their earthly journey.

Silence

Light of the world:
shine in our darkness.

We join our prayers with those of Mary,
who showed her Son to the Wise Men:
Hail, Mary . . .

We pray to the Lord, in silence,
for our own needs and cares.

Silence

Celebrant
Father, we commend our lives
to your loving care,
through Christ our Lord.
Amen.

THE BAPTISM OF THE LORD

Jesus is baptised, and God confirms his identity and his calling.

Celebrant
Let us pray to the God
who calls us each by name.

Reader
We pray for all baptised Christians
to live out their calling in loving and holy lives.
We pray for those preparing
for Baptism and Confirmation;
for parents and godparents
to be given the grace and perseverance
to keep faithfully the promises made.

Silence

Come, Holy Spirit:
fill our lives.

We pray for peace and integrity
in all our dealings as individuals,
and in local, national and international conflicts;
for openness to hear God's wisdom
and courage to follow his lead.

Silence

Come, Holy Spirit:
fill our lives.

We pray for harmony and understanding
in our relationships with family and neighbours;
for the willingness both to give and to receive,
for the generosity of forgiving love.

Silence

Come, Holy Spirit:
fill our lives.

We pray for those whose weariness or pain
makes it difficult for them to pray;
may they sense the support and love
of the Church of God.

Silence

Come, Holy Spirit:
fill our lives.

We pray for those whose souls
have left behind their frail and broken bodies
and can now fly freely to live in God's company
for the whole of eternity.
May their loved ones be blessed and comforted
and may we all be brought
to share the joy of heaven.

Silence

Come, Holy Spirit:
fill our lives.

Now we join our prayers with those of Mary,
the Mother of Jesus:
Hail, Mary . . .

In the silence of God's attentive love,
we name those we know
who are in any particular need.

Silence

Celebrant
Father, confident in your love,
we ask these things
through Christ our Lord.
Amen.

First Sunday of Lent

Following his baptism, Jesus is severely tempted out in the desert,
and shows us how to overcome temptation.

Celebrant
As children of our heavenly Father,
who knows us so well and loves us completely,
let us pray.

Reader
We pray for the Church
as it struggles to steer a straight course
true to the Lord's calling.
We pray for wisdom and courage,
honesty and the willingness to be vulnerable.

Silence

Father, lead us not into temptation:
but deliver us from evil.

Knowing our weakness in the face of temptation,
we ask for strength and protection
so that, though we stumble,
we shall not fall headlong.

Silence

Father, lead us not into temptation:
but deliver us from evil.

We pray for all those
who are fighting temptation
and finding it difficult to resist.
We ask that they may be helped to see clearly,
and be equipped with all they need
to choose what is right.

Silence

Father, lead us not into temptation:
but deliver us from evil.

We pray for those we love,
whose company we enjoy.
We pray too for those who irritate us
and those whom we annoy.

Silence

Father, lead us not into temptation:
but deliver us from evil.

We stand alongside all those who suffer,
all whose lives are in chaos or despair,
and all who live in the dark prison of guilt.
We pray for reassurance and peace,
understanding and compassion.

Silence

Father, lead us not into temptation:
but deliver us from evil.

We pray for the dying,
especially the unnoticed and despised.
We pray for those who have gone through death
and now see the Lord face to face,
that they may receive his merciful forgiveness
and know the joy of living with him for ever.

Silence

Father, lead us not into temptation:
but deliver us from evil.

Now we join our prayers with those of Mary,
the Mother of Jesus:
Hail, Mary . . .

Together in silence,
we name any known to us
with particular needs or burdens.

Silence

Celebrant
Father, we offer you our prayers
in trust and love.
Through Jesus Christ our Lord.
Amen.

SECOND SUNDAY OF LENT

God's glory transfigures Jesus as he prays on the mountain. Our lives,
too, can become increasingly radiant as the Spirit transforms us.

Celebrant
As God's people,
let us pray to him now.

Reader
We long to shine with the Lord's light.
May our hearts be set on fire with love for him
and for one another.

Silence

May our lives proclaim:
that the Lord our God is holy.

We pray for lives of light among the darkness
of injustice, corruption and despair;
may those who are already shining
in dark places all over the world
be strengthened.

Silence

May our lives proclaim:
that the Lord our God is holy.

May the Lord come into our homes
and make them places of welcome
where his love is woven
into all our relationships.

Silence

May our lives proclaim:
that the Lord our God is holy.

May those who have to suffer physical pain
or mental and emotional anguish
be given courage

and enabled to draw on the resources of the Spirit
that can transform all our pain and sorrow.

Silence

May our lives proclaim:
that the Lord our God is holy.

May all who have come to the point of death
be welcomed into the kingdom
of everlasting light.
May those who miss their physical presence be comforted,
and may we all be brought to spend eternity
in the radiance of the presence of God.

Silence

May our lives proclaim:
that the Lord our God is holy.

We make our prayer with Mary,
faithful Mother of Jesus:
Hail, Mary . . .

Knowing that God our Father
hears the prayers of his children,
we pray in silence
our own individual petitions.

Silence

Celebrant
Father, we ask all this
through Christ our Lord.
Amen.

THIRD SUNDAY OF LENT

*The great 'I AM' calls people in every generation to repent
so that God's kingdom can be established and grow.*

Celebrant
Remembering the faithfulness of God our Father,
let us pray to him now.

Reader
God our Father is the God of Abraham,
God of Isaac, God of Jacob;
we thank him for his love and faithfulness
in every generation.
We pray for the Church – the community of faith –
for its leaders and teachers, for all the baptised;
may we hear God's word and will for us,
and have the grace to act on it.

Silence

Lead us:
Heavenly Father, lead us.

God our Father is God of the present,
the past and the future;
we pray that his kingdom of love may come
in every place and every heart,
to bring the healing and hope
which he alone can give.

Silence

Lead us:
Heavenly Father, lead us.

May God our Father teach us to be family;
may he be present in our homes,
not reserved for some special place
but in every room and relationship.

Silence

Lead us:
Heavenly Father, lead us.

We pray that the Lord of peace
may anoint the crushed and oppressed
with the balm of his presence,
to uphold and encourage,
to redeem and transform.

Silence

Lead us:
Heavenly Father, lead us.

We commend to the Lord of life
our own loved ones who have died,
in the sure knowledge that death to this life
is not the final end many fear
but the gateway to eternal life.

Silence

Lead us:
Heavenly Father, lead us.

We pray with Mary,
who heard and believed God's promises:
Hail, Mary . . .

In the stillness of our hearts let us pour out
to our listening God
whatever hangs heavily on our hearts
or uplifts us in thankfulness.

Silence

Merciful Father,
we ask you to hear our prayers
which we make through Christ our Lord.
Amen.

FOURTH SUNDAY OF LENT

Be reconciled with God. He is waiting to welcome us.

Celebrant
Gathered together as children in God's family,
let us pray.

Reader
We pray for the insight and discernment we need
in our church community.
May we learn to have a greater love for the Lord
as we learn to live and work in harmony,
focused on him and not on our divisions.

Silence

God our Father:
supply our needs.

Into the unease and weariness of our world
may the Lord pour the reality and wholesome truth we need,
that we may learn mutual trust
and support one another in love.

Silence

God our Father:
supply our needs.

Into the laughter and tears of family life
may the Lord pour the freshness of his living presence,
as we work at our relationships
and deepen our love for one another.

Silence

God our Father:
supply our needs.

Into the loneliness and pain
of those who feel rejected and unvalued
may the Lord pour his compassion and reassurance,

that each person may know
the full extent of his love for them.

Silence

God our Father:
supply our needs.

May the dying know,
and find comfort and hope in the Lord,
and may those who have died in faith
live for ever in the beauty of his holiness.

Silence

God our Father:
supply our needs.

Mary opened her life
to the loving power of God;
we make our prayer with her:
Hail, Mary . . .

We know that our merciful Father hears us;
let us pray in silence now
for our individual needs.

Silence

Celebrant
Father, hear our prayers,
through Christ our Lord.
Amen.

FIFTH SUNDAY OF LENT

It is not God's wish to condemn anyone,
but he longs for us to turn to him and live.

Celebrant
God is present with us now.
Let us bring him our prayers and concerns
for the Church and for the world.

Reader
We pray that the loving Lord
may continue to breathe his life into the Church,
so that we may speak his love to the world
and be willing to suffer and prepared for sacrifice.

Silence

Lord, through your love:
transform our lives.

We pray that the loving Lord
may breathe his peace into the world,
so that we may work together co-operatively,
sensitive to one another's needs and differences.

Silence

Lord, through your love:
transform our lives.

We pray that the loving Lord
may breathe his patience and forgiveness
into our homes and all our relationships,
so that we may learn
to cherish and respect one another,
and act with generosity.

Silence

Lord, through your love:
transform our lives.

We pray that the loving Lord
may breathe his encouragement
into every suffering and every sadness,
so that the dark and painful times
become places of strong spiritual growth.

Silence

Lord, through your love:
transform our lives.

We pray that the loving Lord
may breathe his welcome
deep into the souls of the dying,
so that death is only the door
leading to the joy of eternal life.

Silence

Lord, through your love:
transform our lives.

We make our prayer with Mary,
who knew the fullness of God's merciful love:
Hail, Mary . . .

Confident in God's forgiving love,
we pray our personal petitions
to him in silence now.

Silence

Celebrant
Father, accept these prayers,
helping us to follow
your example of forgiveness,
and to love others as you love us.
Through Christ our Lord.
Amen.

PALM (PASSION) SUNDAY

As Jesus rides into Jerusalem on a donkey, and the crowds welcome him,
we sense both the joy at the Messiah being acclaimed, and the heaviness
of his suffering which follows. Jesus' mission is drawing to its fulfilment.

Celebrant
As we recall Jesus entering Jerusalem,
let us gather our thoughts to pray.

Reader
As the crowds welcomed Jesus,
we pray that many more will welcome him
into their hearts and lives over the coming year.
We pray for opportunities to spread the good news
and courage to take them.

Silence

Lord, you are our God:
we welcome you!

We recall the donkey Jesus rode on,
and we pray for that real humility in our hearts
which treats status and image casually,
and truth and loving service seriously.

Silence

Lord, you are our God:
we welcome you!

The children sang and shouted in praise;
we pray for the children in our homes,
our city and our land.
May we not fail them
in the support and teaching they need.

Silence

Lord, you are our God:
we welcome you!

The crowds were responding
to the healing love
they had seen in action in Jesus.
In our love and prayer
we now bring all those we would have brought to Jesus
for healing and help.
May they be given comfort and reassurance,
wholeness and hope.

Silence

Lord, you are our God:
we welcome you!

Jesus knew he was riding to his death.
We pray for all on that last journey,
especially those burdened with fear and guilt.
We commend to God's eternal love all who have died.

Silence

Lord, you are our God:
we welcome you!

We make our prayer with Mary,
who shared her Son's sorrows:
Hail, Mary . . .

Together in silence,
we name those known to us
who need our prayers.

Silence

Celebrant
Father, hear our prayer;
may we praise you not only with our voices
but in the lives we lead.
We ask this through Christ our Lord.
Amen.

EASTER DAY

It is true. Jesus is alive for all time.
The Lord of life cannot be held by death. God's victory over
sin and death means that new life for us is a reality.

Celebrant
With joy in our hearts,
come, let us pray together.

Reader
We remember with gratitude
the presence of the Church
in remote and highly populated areas
all over the world.
We pray for all other Christians rejoicing today
in the wonder of the Resurrection.

Silence

Life-giving God:
give us new life in you.

We pray that we may recognise the risen Lord
as we walk through our days,
and we ask that he may remove anything
which blurs our spiritual vision.

Silence

Life-giving God:
give us new life in you.

We pray for the courage to speak out
against injustice and oppression;
we pray that our leaders may establish and uphold
right values and sensitive legislation.

Silence

Life-giving God:
give us new life in you.

We pray that those of our families and friends
who have not yet met the risen Lord
may be drawn into his company and introduced,
so that they can enjoy his faithfulness and love.

Silence

Life-giving God:
give us new life in you.

We remember those whose lives
are filled with pain, anxiety or sorrow,
and ask that the risen Lord may come alongside them
and speak their name.

Silence

Life-giving God:
give us new life in you.

With the words of Resurrection fresh in our minds,
we commend to the Father's eternal love
those who have died,
that they may live with him for ever.

Silence

Life-giving God:
give us new life in you.

We join our prayers with those of Mary,
in her Easter joy:
Hail, Mary . . .

In and through the power of the risen Lord,
we make our private petitions
and thanksgivings.

Silence

Celebrant
Father, in grateful thanks,
we pray we may be worthy
of all your gifts and blessings.
Hear our prayer through Christ, our risen Lord.
Amen.

SECOND SUNDAY OF EASTER

Having seen Jesus in person, the disciples are convinced
of the Resurrection. We too can meet him personally.

Celebrant
In the knowledge that God is here present with us,
let us pray.

Reader
We pray for our bishops, priests and deacons,
in their demanding ministry of love,
that they may be given all the support,
grace and anointing they need.

Silence

Open our eyes, Lord:
to see things your way.

We pray for the gifts of discernment and integrity
among all those who govern, advise and lead.
May all self-centred ambition be cleared away
so that our leaders are free to serve.

Silence

Open our eyes, Lord:
to see things your way.

Whenever we have eye contact with family, friends,
neighbours or colleagues,
we pray that the Lord may be there in that communication,
and remind us of our calling to love one another.

Silence

Open our eyes, Lord:
to see things your way.

We call to mind those whose eyes are wet with tears
or tense with pain.

May they sense the Lord's reassuring love
which can bring us through the darkest of valleys.

Silence

Open our eyes, Lord:
to see things your way.

Jesus is the firstfruit of the new and eternal life.
In gratitude for the privilege
of knowing them here on earth,
we pray for those
who have recently walked through death
into that promise.

Silence

Open our eyes, Lord:
to see things your way.

Together with Mary,
the Mother of our Redeemer,
we make our prayer:
Hail, Mary . . .

In the name of the risen Lord,
we name our own particular cares
and concerns.

Silence

Celebrant
Father, we know that you are here present;
hear the prayers we make,
confident of your love.
Through Christ our Lord.
Amen.

THIRD SUNDAY OF EASTER

Those who know Jesus and recognise that he is the anointed Saviour are commissioned to go out as his witnesses to proclaim the good news.

Celebrant
Let us gather with our prayers
before the God who knows each of us by name.

Reader
We pray for the newly baptised
and those who have recently returned to the Lord.
As the Church, may we support them well
and delight in them as members together
of the Body of Christ.

Silence

Here I am, Lord:
send me!

We pray for strength and protection
against all hypocrisy and double standards
in our society.
We pray for a spirit of genuine service
among all who lead and in all areas
where we have authority.

Silence

Here I am, Lord:
send me!

We pray that our homes and our relationships
may be places where people know,
by the way we look at them and treat them,
that they are valued, cherished
and respected for who they are.

Silence

Here I am, Lord:
send me!

As we call to mind all who have learned
to regard themselves with contempt,
we pray that the Lord may draw near to them
and whisper their true name,
so that they discern the truth
of his love and respect for them.

Silence

Here I am, Lord:
send me!

We pray for the dying
and those who have recently died,
commending them to the joy
and safe-keeping of God's love.

Silence

Here I am, Lord:
send me!

We share Mary's Easter joy
as we join our prayers with hers:
Hail, Mary . . .

In silence filled with love,
we name our particular prayer burdens.

Silence

Celebrant
Father, may we, who confess Christ as Lord,
live in his strength.
Through the same Christ our Lord.
Amen.

FOURTH SUNDAY OF EASTER

Jesus, the Good Shepherd, leads his flock into eternal life.

Celebrant
As members together of the Body of Christ,
let us pray to the true and living God.

Reader
We pray for the nurture
of each member of the Church;
for the newly baptised and for all
in ordained and lay ministry,
that our love for one another may show
as we work for the coming of the kingdom.

Silence

Direct our hearts, O Lord:
to love you more and more.

We pray for the gift of discernment,
so that we recognise God's presence,
and reverence his face
in the faces of those we meet.

Silence

Direct our hearts, O Lord:
to love you more and more.

We pray for our civil rulers
and all those who govern our country
and make its laws,
that we may act responsibly and with compassion,
attentive to real needs and good values.

Silence

Direct our hearts, O Lord:
to love you more and more.

We pray particularly for homes
filled with suspicion and envy,

and ask for the healing of old hurts,
together with hope and perseverance
as people set out on paths of reconciliation.

Silence

Direct our hearts, O Lord:
to love you more and more.

We pray for those whose capacity for trust and love
has been damaged by other people's sin.
We long for the healing and forgiving power of the Spirit,
so that all who are imprisoned by their past
may walk freely with the Lord.

Silence

Direct our hearts, O Lord:
to love you more and more.

We pray for those who have recently passed
through death,
that they may be judged with mercy,
so that, made whole in God's love,
they may know the joy of eternal life.

Silence

Direct our hearts, O Lord:
to love you more and more.

We pray with Mary,
Mother of the Good Shepherd:
Hail, Mary . . .

In a time of silence,
we share with God our Father
our personal burdens, joys and sorrows.

Silence

Celebrant
Father, hear our prayer;
in joy may we follow the way of Christ,
who alone has the words of eternal life.
Through the same Christ our Lord.
Amen.

FIFTH SUNDAY OF EASTER

*Christ, breaking through the barrier of sin and death, allows us to break
into an entirely new way of living which continues into eternity.*

Celebrant
It is God's love that has drawn us here together.
Let us pray to him now.

Reader
Wherever Christians are fussing and arguing,
living outside the Father's will,
we pray for a deep cleansing, healing and renewing,
so that we may truly be the Body of Christ in our world.

Silence

Lord, you show us:
what loving really means.

Wherever injustice stifles human growth,
and selfish ambition distorts leadership,
we pray for right and good government
throughout the world,
born of wisdom and humility.

Silence

Lord, you show us:
what loving really means.

As we watch our children growing,
may they learn from our example
to grow more loving
in the ways we deal with conflict,
approach difficulties,
and address the needs of those we meet.

Silence

Lord, you show us:
what loving really means.

In the places of long-term pain
and sudden shock,
of weariness, disappointment and fear,
we pray for peace which only God can give
and the comfort which speaks of hope.

Silence

Lord, you show us:
what loving really means.

May the physical death of those we now recall
be nothing less than the gateway
to a new and lasting life in God's love and protection.

Silence

Lord, you show us:
what loving really means.

We join our prayers with those of Mary,
whose life was guided by love:
Hail, Mary . . .

In silence,
we make our private petitions to God,
who knows all our needs.

Silence

Celebrant
Father, confident in your boundless love,
we place these prayers before you.
Through Christ our Lord.
Amen.

SIXTH SUNDAY OF EASTER

The continuing presence of God, as Holy Spirit, leads us,
as Jesus promised, into a personally guided outreach to all nations.

Celebrant
Drawn by the Holy Spirit,
we have arrived at this moment,
when we can pray together for the Church
and for the world.

Reader
As members of the Church in this generation,
we ask for guidance and blessing
for all our deacons, priests and bishops,
and all in training for lay and ordained ministry.
As the people of God, we ask for the gifts we need
for the work we are called to do.

Silence

Lord, you are with us:
every step of the way.

This fragile, vulnerable planet is so beautiful,
and in such need of guidance;
we pray for a deeper valuing
of our universe and of one another;
for the kingdom to come on earth as in heaven.

Silence

Lord, you are with us:
every step of the way.

May our homes be centres of love,
acceptance and welcome;
we pray that the Spirit will make his home among us
in each room and each relationship.

Silence

Lord, you are with us:
every step of the way.

We pray for all who are weighed down
with doubts, fears and misgivings;
all who are haunted by the past
or scared by the future.
We ask for them awareness of the Spirit's constant presence
and the courage he brings.

Silence

Lord, you are with us:
every step of the way.

As we remember those
whose earthly life has come to an end,
we pray that they, and we in our turn,
may be received into heaven
and live for ever in divine light.

Silence

Lord, you are with us:
every step of the way.

We make our prayer with Mary,
tranquil Mother of Jesus:
Hail, Mary . . .

Upheld by God's peace,
we pray now in silence
for any needs known to us personally.

Silence

Celebrant
Heavenly Father, accept our prayers
through Christ our Lord.
Amen.

THE ASCENSION OF THE LORD

*Having bought back our freedom with the giving of his life,
Jesus enters into the full glory to which he is entitled.*

Celebrant
As we celebrate together, let us pray together.

Reader
As we celebrate this festival
of Jesus' entry into heaven as Saviour and Lord,
we pray for unity in the Church
and reconciliation and renewed vision.

Silence

God of love, both heaven and earth:
are full of your glory.

We pray that the God of our making
may draw us deeper
into the meaning of life.

Silence

God of love, both heaven and earth:
are full of your glory.

We pray for all farewells and homecomings
among our families and in our community,
and for all who have lost touch with loved ones
and long for reunion.

Silence

God of love, both heaven and earth:
are full of your glory.

We pray for those who are full of tears,
and cannot imagine being happy again;
we pray for the hardened and callous,
whose inner hurts have never yet been healed.
We pray for wholeness and comfort and new life.

Silence

God of love, both heaven and earth:
are full of your glory.

We commend to God's eternal love
those we remember who have died,
and we pray too for those
who miss their physical presence.

Silence

God of love, both heaven and earth:
are full of your glory.

We make our prayer with Mary,
sharing her joy at her Son's Ascension:
Hail, Mary . . .

We pray in silence, now,
for our own particular needs and concerns.

Silence

Celebrant
Father, accept our prayers;
fit us for heaven,
to live with you for ever.
Through Christ our Lord.
Amen.

SEVENTH SUNDAY OF EASTER

Jesus lives for all time in glory; we can live the
fullness of Resurrection life straightaway.

Celebrant
Let us pray to the God who gives us so much
and loves us so completely.

Reader
We pray for a fresh outpouring of the Spirit
in all areas of the Church,
till our lives are so changed for good
that people notice and are drawn to the Lord.

Silence

We are your people:
and you are our God.

We pray for godly leaders and advisers
all over the world,
and for the courage to speak out
against injustice and evil.

Silence

We are your people:
and you are our God.

We pray for those affected
by our behaviour and our conversation,
that we may in future
encourage one another by all we say and do.

Silence

We are your people:
and you are our God.

We pray for those as yet unborn,
that the good news will reach them too;
we pray for those who have rejected God

because of the behaviour of his followers;
we pray for all who have lost their way.

Silence

We are your people:
and you are our God.

We pray for the dying,
especially those who are unprepared or frightened.
May all who have died in faith
be welcomed into the kingdom.

Silence

We are your people:
and you are our God.

We join our prayers with those of Mary,
who was filled with the Holy Spirit:
Hail, Mary . . .

In silence, we pray to the Lord
for our own intentions.

Silence

Celebrant
Father, trusting in your love
we lay these prayers before you
through Christ, our Lord.
Amen.

PENTECOST

*As Jesus promised, the Holy Spirit is poured out
on the apostles and the Church is born.*

Celebrant
As the Spirit enables us,
let us gather ourselves to pray.

Reader
May all Church leaders,
ordained ministers and the laity
be filled to overflowing
with love for all God's people,
and kindled with fresh zeal
for spreading the good news of the Gospel.

Silence

Spirit of the living God:
fall afresh on us.

May all those negotiating for peace
in the delicate areas of national conflict,
industrial disputes and entrenched bitterness,
be blessed with the peace of God,
tranquil and patient beneath the pressures.

Silence

Spirit of the living God:
fall afresh on us.

In our homes and places of work,
our schools and hospitals,
may there always be time
for the warmth of loving concern
and the comfort of being valued.

Silence

Spirit of the living God:
fall afresh on us.

May all rescue workers be strengthened and kept safe;
may all who are trapped in damaged bodies or minds,
in poverty or tyranny, in earthquakes, floods or storms,
be brought to freedom and safety
and be aware of God's love for them.

Silence

Spirit of the living God:
fall afresh on us.

We pray for those who have died
and all who mourn their going;
may the fears of the dying be calmed.

Silence

Spirit of the living God:
fall afresh on us.

The Holy Spirit came down on Mary,
and with her we pray:
Hail, Mary . . .

Alive to the Holy Spirit,
we name those we know
who are in any particular need.

Silence

Celebrant
Father, accept these prayers
through Christ our Lord.
Amen.

TRINITY SUNDAY

The unique nature of God is celebrated today,
as we reflect on the truth that God is Creator,
Redeemer and Life-giver.

Celebrant
Let us pray to the Father,
in the power of the Holy Spirit,
through Jesus, the Son.

Reader
We pray for all theologians
and those who teach the faith
throughout the Church.
We pray for godly wisdom and human insight.

Silence

Holy God:
help us to know you more.

We pray for peace and co-operation,
harmony and mutual respect
in all our dealings with one another
locally, nationally and internationally.

Silence

Holy God:
help us to know you more.

We pray for those who depend on us,
and those on whom we depend,
for our physical and spiritual needs.
May we be enabled to honour one another
as children of God's making.

Silence

Holy God:
help us to know you more.

We pray for those who feel fragmented;
and for those forced to live apart from loved ones
through war, political unrest,
natural disasters or poverty.
We commend their pain
to the comforting of the Spirit.

Silence

Holy God:
help us to know you more.

We remember those who told us of God
through their words and lives;
we think of those who have died in faith
and ask that we may share with them
the joy of God's presence for ever.

Silence

Holy God:
help us to know you more.

Joining Mary, the Mother of our Lord,
we make our prayer:
Hail, Mary . . .

We pray in silence
to our heavenly Father
for our own personal intentions.

Silence

Celebrant
God our Father, hear our prayer;
may we be led by the Spirit
to a deeper knowledge of you.
Through Christ our Lord.
Amen.

CORPUS CHRISTI

*Jesus is the Living Bread, who brings us
eternal life through Communion with him.*

Celebrant
Gathered as the Body of Christ,
let us pray together to our heavenly Father.

Reader
As we celebrate Christ's sacramental presence among us,
we rejoice that we can feed on him
and be nourished with his life.
We pray that the people of God
in every part of the world
may grow in holiness and love.

Silence

Feed us, Father:
with the Living Bread.

We pray for those who know deep spiritual hunger
and for the spiritually complacent;
for a world where loneliness and fear
distrust Christ's promise of hope;
for the kingdom of God to come.

Silence

Feed us, Father:
with the Living Bread.

We pray that through our feeding
the communities we live and work in
may be blessed and nourished;
that our homes may be places of prayer,
and that we may have the courage to be vulnerable.

Silence

Feed us, Father:
with the Living Bread.

We pray for all who receive Communion
in hospital or in their own homes;
that they may find strength and healing
through encountering Christ's love.

Silence

Feed us, Father:
with the Living Bread.

We pray for those whose earthly lives
have come to an end,
that in God's eternity they may find
lasting peace and joy.

Silence

Feed us, Father:
with the Living Bread.

We make our prayers with Mary,
who brought the Living Bread into the world:
Hail, Mary . . .

Let us be still in the presence of God
and bring to him the needs and concerns
that weigh on our hearts.

Silence

Celebrant
Heavenly Father,
you nourish us by the body and blood of Jesus,
so that we can share the life of heaven,
both now and at the end of time.
Hear our prayers and provide for us all.
Amen.

SECOND SUNDAY OF THE YEAR

*As a marriage celebrates the beginning of a changed, new life for
the bride and groom, so our loving, faithful God has chosen us
and is ready to transform our lives for the good of the world.*

Celebrant
Drawn by God's love and constant faithfulness to us,
let us pray.

Reader
We pray for all those who would love to believe
but cannot yet trust in the living God.
We pray for those who have rejected God
because of the unloving behaviour of his followers.

Silence

Fill us, Lord:
fill us to the brim.

We pray for all who give orders
and have influence over other people.
We pray that all peoples may be led justly
and with sensitivity.

Silence

Fill us, Lord:
fill us to the brim.

We pray for all our relationships
which need God's transforming love;
we pray for those we irritate and upset
and those who have hurt and upset us.

Silence

Fill us, Lord:
fill us to the brim.

We pray for those whose lives feel empty
and lacking real meaning.
We pray for those whose frailty, pain or illness
makes it difficult to pray.

Silence

Fill us, Lord:
fill us to the brim.

We pray for those who are dying
and those who have completed their life on earth,
that they may be brought to peace
and everlasting joy.

Silence

Fill us, Lord:
fill us to the brim.

We join our prayers with those of Mary,
chosen Mother of our Lord:
Hail, Mary . . .

In silence,
as God our Father listens with love,
we name our own particular cares and concerns.

Silence

Celebrant
God our Father, hear our prayer;
may the richness of your transforming Spirit
refresh and renew our lives.
Through Christ our Lord.
Amen.

THIRD SUNDAY OF THE YEAR

The meaning of the scriptures is revealed to the people.

Celebrant
Let us still our bodies and our minds
as we pray together to the Father.

Reader
As we call to mind
that we are members of the worldwide Church,
we pray for those who are insulted
or persecuted for our shared faith.
We stand alongside them now.

Silence

Open our ears, Lord:
and teach us to listen to you.

We pray that all of us
who inhabit planet Earth in this age
may learn to hear again
and respond to God's voice of creative love.

Silence

Open our ears, Lord:
and teach us to listen to you.

We pray that wherever materialism
or stress or sorrow or sin
have deafened us to God's will,
we may be prompted to put things right.

Silence

Open our ears, Lord:
and teach us to listen to you.

We pray that our homes may be places
where the Lord is welcomed and recognised
through the good and the troubled times.

Silence

Open our ears, Lord:
and teach us to listen to you.

We pray for all who are ill, injured or sad.
May the Spirit show us how we can help,
and give them a real sense
of his comforting presence.

Silence

Open our ears, Lord:
and teach us to listen to you.

We remember those who have travelled through life
and now have gone through death into eternity.
We give thanks for their lives
and commend them to the Lord's safekeeping.
May he prepare us all, through our living, for eternal life.

Silence

Open our ears, Lord:
and teach us to listen to you.

We pray with Mary,
Mother of the Church:
Hail, Mary . . .

We make our own personal petitions
in silence, now,
to God our loving Father.

Silence

Celebrant
Father, we ask you to hear our prayers,
through Christ our Lord.
Amen.

Fourth Sunday of the Year

As a prophet, Jesus' work is to proclaim the reign of God's love,
not only to the Jewish people but to the whole world.

Celebrant
Let us pray to our loving and faithful God.

Reader
We pray that the Church may be noticeable by its loving;
that all Christians may be remarkable
for their caring and joyful serving
without restrictions or boundaries.

Silence

Loving Father:
hear our prayer.

We pray that through the power of love
conflicts may be resolved, injustices righted,
corruption cleansed and revenge dissolved,
for the world's healing.

Silence

Loving Father:
hear our prayer.

We pray that our homes may be training grounds
for the selfless loving which gives and forgives,
and never ends.

Silence

Loving Father:
hear our prayer.

We pray that fears may be calmed
and the anxious reassured;
that all in pain may be comforted
and restored to wholeness.

Silence

Loving Father:
hear our prayer.

We pray that through Christ's deathless love
those who have died may be forgiven
and brought to eternal life.

Silence

Loving Father:
hear our prayer.

Encouraged by Mary's example of love,
we join our prayers with hers:
Hail, Mary . . .

In the silence of God's attentive love,
we name those we know
who are in any particular need.

Silence

Celebrant
God our Father, hear these prayers;
give us all those qualities of faith, hope and love
which last for ever.
Through Christ our Lord.
Amen.

FIFTH SUNDAY OF THE YEAR

God calls his people and commissions them.

Celebrant
Let us pray together in the presence of our God.

Reader
We pray for all who have been called
to be workers in God's harvest,
searching for the lost and loving them
into the kingdom.
We pray for those who teach God's love,
both by word and by the way they live.

Silence

Here I am, Lord:
ready for your service!

We pray for those in authority
and in positions of power,
that under their leadership
there may be mutual respect, integrity and justice.
We pray for discernment
to see where injustice needs righting
and when we need to speak out.

Silence

Here I am, Lord:
ready for your service!

We pray for families suffering poverty
or financial difficulties,
for families full of tension and disagreement,
and for families coping with grief or separation.
We pray for the extended families represented here.
We pray for better awareness
of how our behaviour affects others.

Silence

Here I am, Lord:
ready for your service!

We pray for those who have been working all night
and all who work long hours in poor conditions.
We pray for those who have no work
and feel rejected.
We pray for any resisting
what God is calling them into.

Silence

Here I am, Lord:
ready for your service!

We pray for those who have died
and those who grieve for the loss of their company.
We ask for the opportunity to prepare for death
by the way we live from now on.

Silence

Here I am, Lord:
ready for your service!

Remembering Mary's special vocation,
we join our prayer with hers:
Hail, Mary . . .

As God's stillness fills our hearts,
we pray for any needs
known to us personally.

Silence

Celebrant
Heavenly Father, hear us,
give us strength and dedication
to offer ourselves to do his will.
Through Christ our Lord.
Amen.

Sixth Sunday of the Year

The challenges and rewards of living by faith.

Celebrant
Knowing our need of God,
let us pray.

Reader
We bring to mind our Church
both here in *(name of town)* and throughout the world.
It is for right values and right priorities
that we pray, in all we decide and do.

Silence

Lord our God:
in you we put our trust.

We bring to mind all who lead and govern,
and all meetings where important decisions are made.
We pray that justice and mercy are upheld
in line with the Father's loving will.

Silence

Lord our God:
in you we put our trust.

We bring to mind our circle of family and friends
with whom we share the good
and the difficult times.
We pray for the grace to discern more readily
the good in each person
and the gifts they have to offer.

Silence

Lord our God:
in you we put our trust.

We bring to mind those caught up
in the frenetic pressures of life,

and those who are stressed to breaking point.
We pray for insight and courage to change things.

Silence

Lord our God:
in you we put our trust.

We bring to mind the dying,
especially those who are alone,
and we remember those we know who have died.
May they and we share
in the everlasting joy of God's presence.

Silence

Lord our God:
in you we put our trust.

We make our prayer with Mary,
whose trust in the Lord is our example:
Hail, Mary . . .

Together now in silence,
we pray our individual petitions
to our heavenly Father.

Silence

Celebrant
We commend all our cares
to the God who loves us as his children.
Through Christ our Lord.
Amen.

SEVENTH SUNDAY OF THE YEAR

Jesus teaches us to love our enemies
and forgive those who sin against us.

Celebrant
God remembers our frailty;
let us pray to him now.

Reader
When conflicts threaten to disrupt our fellowship
in the church community,
may the Spirit help us to deal
with our frustrations and anger,
and give us the grace to forgive.

Silence

Father, may we love one another:
as you have loved us.

When the luggage we carry from the past
interferes with our capacity to cope with the present,
may the Spirit heal the damage from our memories
and transform our experiences for good.

Silence

Father, may we love one another:
as you have loved us.

When the differences in cultures
block our understanding of one another
and obstruct the peace process,
may the Spirit broaden our vision
to discern the common ground.

Silence

Father, may we love one another:
as you have loved us.

When the layers of resentment
have turned into rock,
may the Spirit dissolve them
with the rain of loving mercy.

Silence

Father, may we love one another:
as you have loved us.

As those we have known and loved
pass through the gate of death,
may the Lord have mercy on them,
and receive them into the joy of eternal life.

Silence

Father, may we love one another:
as you have loved us.

We join our prayers with those of Mary,
the Mother of our Lord:
Hail, Mary . . .

We pray in silence now
for our own petitions
to God our heavenly Father.

Silence

Celebrant
Father, accept these prayers;
may your love strengthen
and encourage us all.
Through Christ our Lord.
Amen.

Eighth Sunday of the Year

What we think important flows out in the way we speak.

Celebrant
Let us pray to the God
who knows us as we really are
and loves us so much.

Reader
We bring to the Lord
our desire to see him more clearly
and be more honest with him.
We pray that, as members of his Church,
we may be a people of integrity.

Silence

Open our eyes, Lord:
Heal us from blindness.

We grieve with the oppressed and downtrodden,
we long for Christ to govern the nations,
to soften hardened hearts,
to transform our world with his love.

Silence

Open our eyes, Lord:
Heal us from blindness.

We lay before the Lord
all our relationships,
both the fulfilling and the challenging.

Silence

Open our eyes, Lord:
Heal us from blindness.

We remember with affection and love
those who are in pain or distress,
offering our availability for the Lord to use.
We remember any we have hurt

by our words or attitude,
and ask for the courage and wisdom
to help us put things right.

Silence

Open our eyes, Lord:
Heal us from blindness.

We call to mind those
whom death has hidden from our eyes,
but whom we continue to love and cherish,
knowing they are safe in the Father's care.

Silence

Open our eyes, Lord:
Heal us from blindness.

With Mary, the bearer of God's Son,
we make our prayer:
Hail, Mary . . .

In silence now,
we name any known to us
with particular needs or burdens.

Silence

Celebrant
God our Father,
in our weakness may we rely
on your constant and almighty strength.
We ask you to hear our prayer,
through Christ our Lord.
Amen.

Ninth Sunday of the Year

The good news we have been given is not
just for us, but to pass on to the rest of the world.

Celebrant
We have gathered here today
in the company of the true God.
Let us pray to him now.

Reader
We pray for the Lord's blessing and anointing
on all involved with mission and outreach,
both here and abroad, among children and adults,
as they commit themselves
to spreading the good news.

Silence

You are the living God:
let your will be done in us.

We pray for all who have influence and authority,
through their political standing, fame or wealth;
speak into their hearts of righteousness and justice,
integrity and compassion.

Silence

You are the living God:
let your will be done in us.

We pray that we may take seriously
our responsibilities for nurturing our children
and those who do not yet know God's love.
May our living be transformed to reveal that love.

Silence

You are the living God:
let your will be done in us.

We call to mind those in need
of comfort and reassurance,
all in pain and mental anguish.
We pray for the lapsed and the doubting
and those who need the Good News this week.

Silence

You are the living God:
let your will be done in us.

We pray for those who have recently died
and those on that last journey now.
May we all be brought safely to heaven.

Silence

You are the living God:
let your will be done in us.

With Mary, Mother of Jesus,
let us pray:
Hail, Mary . . .

In silence, we pray our individual petitions
to the Lord of all.

Silence

Celebrant
Heavenly Father, we ask you to hear our prayers,
through Christ our Lord.
Amen.

Tenth Sunday of the Year

Our God is full of compassion;
he hears our crying and it is his nature to rescue us.

Celebrant
Let us bring to the God who loves us
our prayers and concerns for the Church
and the world.

Reader
May the God of compassion
take our hearts of stone
and give us feeling hearts,
so that we as the Church
may be more responsive
to the needs and sorrows around us.

Silence

God of love:
show us the Way.

May the God of wisdom
teach all in authority,
inspire those who lead,
protect each nation from evil,
and further each right decision.

Silence

God of love:
show us the Way.

May the God of tenderness
dwell in our homes
through all the times of joy
and all the heartaches and sadness,
teaching us to show one another
the love he shows to us.

Silence

God of love:
show us the Way.

May the God of wholeness
speak into the despair and loneliness
of all who struggle with life and its troubles;
to reassure, affirm and encourage them,
and alert us to ways we can help.

Silence

God of love:
show us the Way.

May the God of peace
be with the dying,
and welcome those who have died in faith
into the full life of the kingdom.

Silence

God of love:
show us the Way.

We make our prayer with Mary,
Mother of our risen Lord:
Hail, Mary . . .

We know our Father is listening;
in silence we bring to him
our own particular needs or burdens.

Silence

Celebrant
God our Father, hear our prayer
and help us to do your will.
Through Christ our Lord.
Amen.

ELEVENTH SUNDAY OF THE YEAR

*God has the authority and the desire to forgive our
sins completely and set us free from guilt.*

Celebrant
Knowing your love for us, Holy God,
we have come before you to pray together.

Reader
We pray for all who have the care of souls,
and are entrusted with helping others to repentance
and giving them good counsel.
We pray for those called to speak God's values,
whatever the danger and regardless of popularity.

Silence

Work in us, Lord:
work in us for good.

We pray for those who refuse
to allow injustice or evil to go unchallenged;
for all who are under pressure
to behave wrongly
or keep quiet about something
they know to be wrong.

Silence

Work in us, Lord:
work in us for good.

We pray for more loving forgiveness
in all our relationships,
for more self-knowledge,
the grace to recognise where we are in the wrong,
and the courage to seek God's forgiveness.

Silence

Work in us, Lord:
work in us for good.

We pray for all imprisoned by guilt, resentment,
bitterness and self-pity,
that they may come to know
the relief of being forgiven.
We pray for all innocent victims,
that their scars may be completely healed.

Silence

Work in us, Lord:
work in us for good.

We pray for those who have died
unprepared to meet the Lord,
and for all who have died in faith.
May the Lord have mercy on us all.

Silence

Work in us, Lord:
work in us for good.

We make our prayer with Mary,
who listened in loving obedience to God:
Hail, Mary . . .

We pray in silence,
making our own petitions
to God our heavenly Father.

Silence

Celebrant
Father, we ask you to hear our prayers
through your Son, Christ our Lord.
Amen.

Twelfth Sunday of the Year

Following Christ means daily taking up our cross.

Celebrant
As followers of Christ, let us pray.

Reader
When following Christ brings danger,
weariness or suffering,
we pray for courage and strength.

Silence

In the shadow of your wings:
we shall be in safety.

When we watch the violence and selfishness
of a bewildered and fearful world,
we know our desperate need for peace.
May Christ's peace transform our world.

Silence

In the shadow of your wings:
we shall be in safety.

When we struggle in our relationships
and ache for those we love,
we pray for guidance, forgiveness
and the grace to go on forgiving.

Silence

In the shadow of your wings:
we shall be in safety.

We pray that into all the suffering, pain and hunger
which cries out from our humanity,
Christ will bring the refreshment of his healing love.

Silence

In the shadow of your wings:
we shall be in safety.

When those we know and love meet death,
and we must let them go,
may they be welcomed into the kingdom
of the Father's eternal peace.

Silence

In the shadow of your wings:
we shall be in safety.

We pray with Mary,
who shared her Son's sorrows:
Hail, Mary . . .

In silence now,
we share with God our Father
our personal burdens, joys and sorrows.

Silence

Celebrant
Father, hear our prayers;
we ask for mercy,
encouragement and support.
Through Christ our Lord.
Amen.

Thirteenth Sunday of the Year

When we are called to follow Jesus,
that means total commitment, with no half-measures.

Celebrant
Holy God, you have called us
to meet and pray together,
and here we are.

Reader
We pray for those called
to lay and ordained ministry in the Church,
and for those at present testing their vocation.
We lay before the Lord the work that needs doing here
and ask him to provide people to do it.

Silence

We ask in Jesus' name:
give us grace to discern your answer.

We pray for those called to serve
in positions of authority and influence;
for all leaders to see true greatness as service
and true strength as humility.

Silence

We ask in Jesus' name:
give us grace to discern your answer.

We pray for those called to marriage,
and those called to the single life,
for parents and grandparents,
sons and daughters,
for acceptance of what we cannot change
and strength to live the Christian life
in our present situation.

Silence

We ask in Jesus' name:
give us grace to discern your answer.

We pray for those whose lives
are full of disappointment,
disillusion and discontent;
for all who struggle with great perseverance
in difficult circumstances.
We pray for strength, encouragement and direction.

Silence

We ask in Jesus' name:
give us grace to discern your answer.

We pray for those called, through death,
into eternal life
and freedom from all their pain and suffering.
May they receive mercy
and be welcomed into the kingdom.

Silence

We ask in Jesus' name:
give us grace to discern your answer.

We make our prayer with Mary,
who committed herself fully to God's will:
Hail, Mary . . .

In loving silence, now,
we make our private petitions.

Silence

Celebrant
Lord and heavenly Father,
as we commit our lives afresh
to your service,
we ask you to hear our prayers.
Through Christ our Lord.
Amen.

Fourteenth Sunday of the Year

In Christ we become a new creation.

Celebrant
Let us bring our cares and concerns
before the God who loves us.

Reader
We pray for more workers
to gather in the harvest of the kingdom;
for our churches to be places of welcome
and wholesome spiritual nurture.

Silence

Use us, Lord:
in the building of your kingdom.

We pray for our nation and the nations of the world;
for an upholding of godly principles and just laws,
for reconciliation, peace and mutual co-operation.

Silence

Use us, Lord:
in the building of your kingdom.

We pray for those among our families and friends
who have no idea of the new life the Lord offers;
we pray for them to discover him
so they may share the joy of living in his love.

Silence

Use us, Lord:
in the building of your kingdom.

We pray for those who are suffering,
for those disfigured by disease or accidents,
for the lonely, the confused and the outcasts.

Silence

Use us, Lord:
in the building of your kingdom.

We pray for the dying, and their loved ones,
for those who have passed through death,
and the families and friends who miss them.
May they be surrounded by the Father's everlasting love.

Silence

Use us, Lord:
in the building of your kingdom.

We pray now with Mary,
serene Mother of our Lord:
Hail, Mary . . .

God our Father loves us;
in silence we pray
our personal petitions to him now.

Silence

Celebrant
Father, knowing that you alone
have the words of eternal life,
we lay our prayers before you.
Through Christ our Lord.
Amen.

FIFTEENTH SUNDAY OF THE YEAR

Straighten your lives out and live by God's standards of love.

Celebrant
Let us pray to God,
knowing we can trust him.

Reader
We pray that as Christians we may take to heart
the need to walk the talk,
and live out what we profess.
We pray that nothing may get so important to us
that it pushes God's values aside.

Silence

Father:
let only your will be done.

We pray that those in authority and power
do not lose touch with the needs of those they serve,
so that the poor and oppressed and vulnerable
are always given value and respect.

Silence

Father:
let only your will be done.

We pray for those in our families
whom we love and have hurt or upset;
we pray too for those who have hurt or upset us,
and ask for God's reconciliation and healing.

Silence

Father:
let only your will be done.

We pray for those who have lost hope
of being rescued, noticed or valued;

for the complacent who cannot see their poverty,
for the prejudiced who mistake blindness for sight.

Silence

Father:
let only your will be done.

We pray for our loved ones
who have reached the moment of death;
we give thanks for the example of their lives
and commend them all to God's safekeeping.

Silence

Father:
let only your will be done.

Mary's example teaches us
the power of loving response;
with her we make our prayer:
Hail, Mary . . .

In the silence of God's stillness,
we name any we know
who especially need our prayer.

Silence

Celebrant
Lord God of love,
we offer you these prayers,
through Christ our Lord.
Amen.

SIXTEENTH SUNDAY OF THE YEAR

Attentive listening is all part of serving.

Celebrant
Our God is always ready to listen.
Let us pray to him now.

Reader
We pray to the Lord
that he may continue to pour out his gifts on the Church,
so that many may be saved
and our faith may grow strong
and bear much fruit.

Silence

God of Love:
we put our trust in you.

We pray to the Lord
that he may look with mercy on the conflicts of our world;
that we may realign our values and goals
until they are in line with his will,
and our laws and expectations
reflect his justice and love.

Silence

God of Love:
we put our trust in you.

We pray to the Lord
that he may bless our homes and families
and all our neighbours and friends;
may we listen to one another with full attention,
and recognise one another's gifts.

Silence

God of Love:
we put our trust in you.

We pray to the Lord
that he may encourage the hesitant,
curb the overpowering,
heal the sick, refresh the exhausted,
soften the hardened hearts,
open the eyes of the complacent,
and comfort all who are sad.

Silence

God of Love:
we put our trust in you.

We pray to the Lord
that he may welcome into eternity
all those who have died in faith;
may we in our turn share with them
the joy of living in his peace for ever.

Silence

God of Love:
we put our trust in you.

We pray with Mary,
who was the first to welcome Jesus:
Hail, Mary . . .

In the silence of God's attentive love,
we pray our private petitions.

Silence

Celebrant
God our Father, hear our prayer;
we ask you to help us fix our lives on you.
Through Christ our Lord.
Amen.

Seventeenth Sunday of the Year

*Keep asking for God's Spirit and he will keep
pouring out his blessing on you.*

Celebrant
Heavenly Father, as you have taught us,
through Jesus,
we come to you in prayer.

Reader
We pray for all who uphold and teach the faith,
for young Christians in schools and universities,
for Christians witnessing to their faith at work,
for all in danger of persecution.
We pray for strength and courage.

Silence

In all things, Father:
let your will be done.

We pray for discernment and wisdom
as we strive for international co-operation
in managing the world's resources;
for perseverance as we work
towards peace and reconciliation.

Silence

In all things, Father:
let your will be done.

We pray for the good sense
in our family and community life
that knows the difference
between generosity and indulgence,
between lenience and neglect of responsibility.

Silence

In all things, Father:
let your will be done.

We pray for all victims of abuse and tyranny,
for all who suffer long-term effects
of torture, war or disease;
we pray for the grace to forgive,
and for healing of body, mind and spirit.

Silence

In all things, Father:
let your will be done.

We pray for those who have died,
and particularly for those
who have no one to mourn their going;
for those who have died unnoticed.
We pray that they may rest in peace for ever.

Silence

In all things, Father:
let your will be done.

Mary's response prepared the way
for our salvation;
we make our prayer with her:
Hail, Mary . . .

In silence filled with love,
we name our particular prayer burdens.

Silence

Celebrant
God our Father,
rejoicing in your tenderness and compassion,
we bring these prayers before you.
Through Christ our Lord.
Amen.

Eighteenth Sunday of the Year

True richness is not material wealth;
true security is not a financial matter.

Celebrant
Let us pray to God our Father,
knowing that we are all precious to him.

Reader
We pray for all those who give
to support the work of the Church;
may the Lord bless our giving,
guide our spending,
and help us to value the true wealth
of his abundant love.

Silence

The Lord is our shepherd:
there is nothing we shall want.

We pray for the world's economy;
for fair management and distribution of resources;
for fair trade and just wages;
for greater awareness and concern about injustice;
for a commitment to our responsibilities
as planet-sharers and earth-dwellers.

Silence

The Lord is our shepherd:
there is nothing we shall want.

We pray for all parents with young children;
may they be blessed and guided in their parenting;
we pray for families in debt;
for those whose homes have been repossessed,
and those whose financial security
makes them forgetful of God's love.

Silence

The Lord is our shepherd:
there is nothing we shall want.

We pray for those who are burdened
with financial worries
and all who struggle to make ends meet,
all over the world;
we pray for the emotionally and spiritually bankrupt,
and those who do not yet know God's love for them.

Silence

The Lord is our shepherd:
there is nothing we shall want.

We pray for those who have died,
and those on that last journey at this moment;
for a merciful judgement
and the everlasting joy of heaven.

Silence

The Lord is our shepherd:
there is nothing we shall want.

We pray with Mary,
who knew the true value of all things:
Hail, Mary . . .

In the silence of our hearts,
we bring to our heavenly Father
our needs and concerns.

Silence

Celebrant
Lord our God,
acknowledging your greatness,
we ask you to accept these prayers,
through Christ our Lord.
Amen.

Nineteenth Sunday of the Year

Have faith in God, and get yourself ready to meet him.

Celebrant
As God's beloved children,
let us come to him and open our hearts to him.

Reader
The Father knows both our gifts as a congregation
and the needs of those in this parish;
we ask him to bless our ministry in this place,
to strengthen and encourage all Church leaders
and to deepen our faith and sure hope.

Silence

Lord our God:
we believe and trust in you.

We pray that the Father may heal our nation
and all the nations
of what is in the past and still corrodes the present,
so that we may build on good foundations
and learn to govern ourselves with honesty,
respect for one another and sensitivity to needs.

Silence

Lord our God:
we believe and trust in you.

We pray that the Father may be present
in the daily living of our homes
and in all our relationships,
and make us more trustworthy in our friendships,
and strengthen our resolve to live our faith in action.

Silence

Lord our God:
we believe and trust in you.

We call to mind all whose capacity to trust
has been damaged;
for those who are victims of injustice or corruption;
for the very young and the very old,
the frail, the vulnerable and the bereaved.

Silence

Lord our God:
we believe and trust in you.

We remember those
who have completed their earthly life in faith
and have now seen the Lord face to face.
May they know the peace of eternity;
we too look forward to sharing that life of joy.

Silence

Lord our God:
we believe and trust in you.

We make our prayer with Mary,
who was ever watchful in God's service:
Hail, Mary . . .

We pray in silence
to God, who knows our needs.

Silence

Celebrant
God our Father, accept our prayers;
as we learn to trust more in your promise,
may we grow to be more like Christ
and reflect the radiance of his love.
Through the same Christ, our Lord.
Amen.

Twentieth Sunday of the Year

When we fix our eyes on Jesus our lives will reflect his nature.

Celebrant
God is close to us as we pray.
He is attentive to us now.

Reader
Whenever the Lord weeps over our harshness,
may his tears melt our hearts of stone.
Whenever he grieves over our double standards,
may we be shocked into honesty again.
May he make us receptive to his teaching,
willing to take risks
and eager to run with our eyes fixed on him.

Silence

Lead us, Lord:
to walk in your ways.

Whenever the news overwhelms us,
may the Lord nudge us to fervent prayer.
Wherever leaders meet to negotiate peace,
may he be present at the conference table.
May he breathe his values into our thinking,
tear down the divisive barriers
and renew us to lead the world into loving.

Silence

Lead us, Lord:
to walk in your ways.

We pray that whenever tempers are frayed
and patience is wearing thin,
the Spirit may give us space
to collect ourselves and try again.
Whenever the demands of family and friends
remind us of our limitations,
may the Spirit minister graciously through our weakness
and teach us the humility of apologising.

Silence

Lead us, Lord:
to walk in your ways.

Whenever people are enveloped by pain
or desolate grief or total exhaustion,
may the Spirit bring refreshment and peace,
tranquillity and hope,
and wherever the grip of the past
prevents free movement into the future,
bring release and healing.

Silence

Lead us, Lord:
to walk in your ways.

We pray for the dying,
especially those who are fearful and distressed;
may they be comforted and reassured
on that last journey.
May those who care for them
and those who mourn their going be blessed.

Silence

Lead us, Lord:
to walk in your ways.

We make our prayer with Mary,
Mother of our Saviour:
Hail, Mary ...

Trustingly we pray in silence
to God our Father,
who considers each one of us special.

Silence

Celebrant
Loving Father, hear our prayers,
through Christ our Lord.
Amen.

TWENTY-FIRST SUNDAY OF THE YEAR

*At the great and final gathering in, it will be a question
of each person's chosen life direction,
and each response to the way of God.*

Celebrant
Trusting not in ourselves but in God's mercy,
let us pray.

Reader
That in all the decisions and activities of the church,
we may be slow to rush ahead of God's guiding
yet quick to follow where he leads.

Silence

In you, O Lord:
we place our trust.

That in all the hardships and dangers of life,
in all the crises, conflicts and injustices,
we may keep clear-sighted and attentive to God's will.

Silence

In you, O Lord:
we place our trust.

That with our friends, neighbours and loved ones,
and those we are tempted to despise or dismiss,
we may have many opportunities
for loving service.

Silence

In you, O Lord:
we place our trust.

That in those who live fearfully,
God may breathe his peace,
and on those who are ill and frail,
he may place healing hands.

Silence

In you, O Lord:
we place our trust.

That God's comfort may surround all
who are dying unrecognised or unnoticed,
and that all who die in God's friendship
may be welcomed into eternity with him.

Silence

In you, O Lord:
we place our trust.

We join our prayers with those of Mary,
our spiritual Mother:
Hail, Mary ...

Confident in God's welcoming love,
we pray in silence now,
for our own particular needs and concerns.

Silence

Celebrant
God our Father, accept these prayers,
through Christ our Lord.
Amen.

Twenty-second Sunday of the Year

When we live God's way, both individually
and as a community, we will be greatly blessed.

Celebrant
Let us do the work of prayer
that God has asked of us.

Reader
As the body constantly breathes,
may the Church, the Body of Christ, constantly pray,
breathing God's life into all its members and activities.

Silence

The Lord is our helper:
we shall not be afraid.

As a new week begins in our world,
may wrong priorities be challenged and adjusted,
may our societies reflect God's concern
for righteousness, true justice and responsive love,
and may all leaders grow in humility,
attentive to the needs of those they serve.

Silence

The Lord is our helper:
we shall not be afraid.

As we call to mind our loved ones,
all who depend on us,
and those on whom we depend,
all with whom we laugh, cry, work or play,
cleanse and refresh our relationships
and give us greater love,
understanding and forgiveness.

Silence

The Lord is our helper:
we shall not be afraid.

We think of those who are in prison,
locked in cells or depression or dysfunctional bodies;
we think of those in hospital wards
and accident centres,
those unable to reach medical help
and those on long waiting-lists for operations;
as we think of them all, we pray for them all.

Silence

The Lord is our helper:
we shall not be afraid.

We remember the dying and those who love them;
we remember those whose earthly life
has come to an end,
and we commend them to God's undying love.

Silence

The Lord is our helper:
we shall not be afraid.

Mindful of Mary's quiet
and prayerful acceptance of God's will,
we join our prayers with hers:
Hail, Mary . . .

In silence, we pray for our own intentions
to God, our loving Father.

Silence

Celebrant
Lord God, giver of all good gifts,
we ask you to hear these prayers.
Through Christ our Lord.
Amen.

TWENTY-THIRD
SUNDAY OF THE YEAR

Following Jesus is expensive –
it costs everything, but it's worth it.

Celebrant
Let us pray to the God who has watched our growing
throughout our lives, and loves us.

Reader
There is nothing hidden from the Lord.
All our thoughts and plans and secret fears
are open to him, even when we try to hide them.
May he give us the courage and strength
to deal with the doubts and misgivings
and fears of his Church,
with the love and mercy
which are part of his nature.

Silence

Gracious God:
in you we can trust.

The Lord feels for the oppressed and the forgotten;
understands the damage which can lead to violence,
the insecurity which can lead to defensiveness,
and the neglect which can lead to lack of control.
We pray that he may heal the nations,
restore what has been lost,
and turn our hearts to discern his will.

Silence

Gracious God:
in you we can trust.

The Lord knows the love inside our hearts for one another
that sings and dances and aches and worries.
We pray that the Spirit may work on us now
in the depth of our being,
and bless our loved ones with a sense of joy.

Silence

Gracious God:
in you we can trust.

The Lord suffers with those who suffer
and weeps with those who weep;
we, too, stand alongside them now
in whatever pain, distress or sorrow
is engulfing them,
and we pray that they may be comforted.

Silence

Gracious God:
in you we can trust.

The Lord's death and resurrection
proclaim the message of hope
amongst the tears of our grieving
for those who have died.
May they be welcomed
into the eternal light of the kingdom.

Silence

Gracious God:
in you we can trust.

We join our prayers with those of Mary,
who spent her life in God's service:
Hail, Mary . . .

In silence, we make our own petitions
to God, who loves us as his own.

Silence

Celebrant
Father, accept our prayers;
all that we are,
and all we are capable of becoming,
we pledge to your service.
Through Christ our Lord.
Amen.

TWENTY-FOURTH
SUNDAY OF THE YEAR

Jesus does not avoid the company of sinners but befriends them.

Celebrant
Let us pray to the God who longs for all to be rescued.

Reader
We pray for our bishops, priests and deacons,
and all who are called
to the different ministries in the Church.
May they be blessed
as they work in the service of the Lord.

Silence

God our shepherd:
all our needs are known to you.

We pray for all peace initiatives
and every genuine attempt at negotiation
in conflict resolution.
May those who govern be governed by the Father's love;
may those who lead be led by the Spirit's directing;
may the whole world come to know its need of Christ.

Silence

God our shepherd:
all our needs are known to you.

We pray for our families and friends,
for those we meet each day and those we seldom see;
may all our loved ones be drawn closer to the Lord.
May he search out those whose faith
is fragile or fragmented.

Silence

God our shepherd:
all our needs are known to you.

As we recall the needs
of those who are sad or lonely,
lost, or afraid of what they have become,
we pray for the knowledge of the Father's love
to wrap warmly around them,
and his living presence
to bring them to a place of safety and hope.

Silence

God our shepherd:
all our needs are known to you.

We pray for those who have recently died;
may they enjoy the eternal life of heaven,
where there is no more pain, sorrow or weariness,
and every tear shall be wiped away.

Silence

God our shepherd:
all our needs are known to you.

We join our prayers with those of Mary,
Mother of our forgiving Lord:
Hail, Mary . . .

Together in silence,
we name those known to us
who especially need our prayer.

Silence

Celebrant
Merciful Father, accept these prayers,
through Christ our Lord.
Amen.

TWENTY-FIFTH SUNDAY OF THE YEAR

If you cannot be trusted with worldly riches,
or even small amounts of money, then you will
not be trusted with spiritual riches either.

Celebrant
As God has taught us, let us pray
for the coming of the kingdom in every situation.

Reader
We pray for the Church to be pure and holy,
alight with God's love and compassion,
and free from behaviour which is unworthy
of God's chosen people.

Silence

God our Father:
let your kingdom come.

We pray for the nations to be wisely governed,
with just laws and a sense of vision
which reflects the best of human nature.
We pray for peace and mutual respect
in each community throughout the world.

Silence

God our Father:
let your kingdom come.

We pray for our homes to be filled with God's love,
so we are happy to put ourselves out for others,
to listen with full attention, and to value one another.
We pray for the strength
to clear away anything in our life-style
which competes with God for our commitment.

Silence

God our Father:
let your kingdom come.

We pray for those who feel neglected
or rejected by society,
that they may know God's love and acceptance of them.
We pray for all those in pain and distress,
that they may be comforted and relieved.

Silence

God our Father:
let your kingdom come.

We pray that the dying may recognise
their need of God and his power to save;
that those who have died may be judged with mercy
and rest in God's peace.

Silence

God our Father:
let your kingdom come.

We pray with Mary, Mother of Jesus:
Hail, Mary . . .

In silence, now,
we pour out to God our Father
any needs and burdens known to us personally.

Silence

Celebrant
Lord God of all creation,
accept these prayers,
through Christ our Lord.
Amen.

Twenty-sixth Sunday of the Year

*Wealth can make us complacent so that we fail
to notice the needs of those around us.*

Celebrant
All our needs are God's concerns.
Let us pray to him now.

Reader
May we be a listening Church,
welcoming to the hesitant,
encouraging to the young,
sensitive to the differences and attentive to the needs.

Silence

God, in mercy:
hear us as we pray.

May we be a caring world,
wise in government,
honest in promises,
far-sighted in the management of resources,
and open-hearted in charitable giving.

Silence

God, in mercy:
hear us as we pray.

May we be a responsible community,
supporting our neighbours and friends,
sharing one another's sorrows and joys,
and opening our homes to the presence of the Lord.

Silence

God, in mercy:
hear us as we pray.

As we remember those
who have asked for our prayers,
we ask that the Lord may take their needs
and provide for them,
take their wounds and heal them,
take their suffering and comfort them.

Silence

God, in mercy:
hear us as we pray.

As we call to mind those who have died,
may they know the welcoming of God's love
into eternal joy.

Silence

God, in mercy:
hear us as we pray.

We make our prayer with Mary,
whose generous heart
was so open to God's will:
Hail, Mary . . .

In silence, let us commend
our own particular needs and thankfulness
to the God of power and mercy.

Silence

Celebrant
Heavenly Father, hear these prayers,
through your Son, Jesus Christ.
Amen.

TWENTY-SEVENTH SUNDAY OF THE YEAR

God hears our distress and our crying, and feels it with us.

Celebrant
Knowing that God hears our prayers,
let us share our concerns with him
for the Church and for the world.

Reader
We pray for all in lay and ordained ministry,
as they labour for the growth
of God's kingdom on earth;
may he keep them strong in the faith,
provide them with the energy and resources they need,
and inspire them daily with his love.

Silence

Lord, you are our hope:
you are our strength.

We pray for all meetings, conventions, and conferences,
for all policy making and planning;
may delicate negotiations be sensitively led,
and painful decisions bravely and wisely taken.

Silence

Lord, you are our hope:
you are our strength.

We pray for those we have upset or angered,
and those who have upset or angered us;
we pray for those who worry us,
and those we love but seldom manage to see.

Silence

Lord, you are our hope:
you are our strength.

We pray for those who are far from home
and those for whom it is too dangerous
to return home;
we pray for the lonely, the unhappy,
those in pain and those convalescing.

Silence

Lord, you are our hope:
you are our strength.

We remember those who have come
to the end of their earthly life,
and for those whose lives feel bleak
and empty without them.
We pray for mercy and peace and comfort.

Silence

Lord, you are our hope:
you are our strength.

We pray with Mary,
whose faith was unfaltering:
Hail, Mary . . .

Trustingly we pray in silence
to our loving God for our own needs and cares.

Silence

Celebrant
Father, as we dedicate ourselves afresh
to serving you,
accept these prayers,
through Christ our Lord.
Amen.

TWENTY-EIGHTH
SUNDAY OF THE YEAR

God can always use even seemingly hopeless situations for good.

Celebrant
God has proclaimed his love for us.
We can trust him with all our cares and concerns.

Reader
We pray that the Church may be healed
of all its splits and divisions,
and grow towards unity.

Silence

Have pity on us, Lord:
you alone can save us.

May our society be mindful of those
who have particular difficulties;
may our laws testify to our sense of justice,
honour and integrity;
may the world's leaders be wisely advised
and honestly motivated.

Silence

Have pity on us, Lord:
you alone can save us.

May the Lord walk in our homes
with gifts of peace, patience, forgiveness and joy;
may he help us through the disappointments and tragedies,
and celebrate with us in all our festivities,
as our most honoured guest.

Silence

Have pity on us, Lord:
you alone can save us.

We pray for all suffering from leprosy
and other infectious and life-threatening diseases;
may the Lord give courage
to the long-term and chronically ill,
and respite to those who are at their wits' end.

Silence

Have pity on us, Lord:
you alone can save us.

We remember those who have died,
and we think of their loved ones, who miss them.
May this earthly death be a birth
into the eternal joy of heaven.

Silence

Have pity on us, Lord:
you alone can save us.

We make our prayer with Mary,
whose heart was full of thanks and praise:
Hail, Mary . . .

Confident in God's welcoming love,
we pray in silence, now,
for any needs known to us personally.

Silence

Celebrant
Heavenly Father, to whom all glory belongs,
accept our prayers, through Christ our Lord.
Amen.

TWENTY-NINTH SUNDAY OF THE YEAR

Don't get side-tracked; always pray and don't give up.

Celebrant
Our help comes from the Lord.
Let us pray to him now.

Reader
We pray for those who teach prayer
and open the Scriptures to others
at schools and colleges, retreat houses,
and conferences,
and in churches and homes all over the world.
We pray that many will find in Scripture
words speaking into their situation
and providing the guidance they need.

Silence

Lord, we love your ways:
our help comes from you.

We pray for those picking their way
through situations of potential conflict and danger;
for law makers and keepers
and all who are oppressed unjustly;
for the leaders of the nations and their people.

Silence

Lord, we love your ways:
our help comes from you.

We pray for the grace to listen to one another
and respond to one another's needs;
we pray for a spirit of co-operation and generosity
in our homes and neighbourhoods.

Silence

Lord, we love your ways:
our help comes from you.

We pray for those who are wrestling with problems
which seem too big to cope with;
for those who have recently received news
that has stunned or appalled them,
and are still in a state of shock.

Silence

Lord, we love your ways:
our help comes from you.

We pray for those who have gone through death,
that they may be judged with mercy
and brought safely into the eternal life of heaven.

Silence

Lord, we love your ways:
our help comes from you.

Encouraged by Mary's prayerful example,
we join our prayer with hers:
Hail, Mary . . .

We pray in silence our own petitions
to God our Father,
who knows all our needs.

Silence

Celebrant
God, our heavenly Father,
bless our lives to your service,
and accept our prayers,
through Christ our Lord.
Amen.

THIRTIETH SUNDAY OF THE YEAR

When we recognise our dependence on God we will
approach him with true humility and accept his gifts with joy.

Celebrant
Let us pray to the God who made us and sustains us.

Reader
We pray for the Church,
with all our faults and failings,
missed opportunities and misunderstandings;
may we be guided
to be truly the Body of Christ on earth.

Silence

God of our making:
have mercy on us.

We lay before the Lord the political issues,
the moral dilemmas and the dreams of peace
that concern our world,
and all who share its resources.
Where we can see no clear way forward
we pray for vision to enable us
to be good stewards of all God provides.

Silence

God of our making:
have mercy on us.

We pray that the Lord may take all our relationships
and drench them in his transforming love,
so that we appreciate one another more,
and value what each has to offer.

Silence

God of our making:
have mercy on us.

We pray for those who feel spiritually dried-up
or emotionally drained;
may the Lord heal and mend
broken bodies and broken hearts,
and provide clear pools of water for those
who are walking the valley of misery and depression.

Silence

God of our making:
have mercy on us.

We pray for those who have run the race
and fought the good fight,
may the Lord have mercy
on all who are at the point of death,
and receive them into his kingdom.

Silence

God of our making:
have mercy on us.

May we learn from the humility of Mary,
as we pray with her to the God of heaven:
Hail, Mary . . .

In silence now,
we make our private petitions to God,
who always hears our prayers of faith.

Silence

Celebrant
Lord God, accept these prayers,
through Christ our Lord.
Amen.

THIRTY-FIRST
SUNDAY OF THE YEAR

Jesus came to search out the lost and save them.
Through him we come to our senses and make our lives clean.

Celebrant
Let us still ourselves in our Father's presence
and tell him what is on our hearts.

Reader
We pray that the Lord may look into us and teach us
to know ourselves more honestly,
to recognise the areas which need cleansing,
and inspire us to live more faithfully and fruitfully
as the people of God.

Silence

Lord, may our lives:
express our love for you.

We pray that parliaments and all places of government
throughout the world may be filled
with a desire for integrity and a determination
to stamp out corruption and deceit.

Silence

Lord, may our lives:
express our love for you.

May the Lord speak his peace and reconciliation
into all family disputes
and hurtful misunderstandings;
and may a spirit of loving community
be nurtured in our neighbourhood,
heightening our awareness of one another's needs.

Silence

Lord, may our lives:
express our love for you.

We pray that the Lord may bring
reassurance and practical help
to those who are close to despair
and those in long-term suffering;
may he use us as instruments of his healing love.

Silence

Lord, may our lives:
express our love for you.

We pray for those
who have faithfully lived out their days;
as we miss their physical presence,
may they be brought into the peace
of God's kingdom.

Silence

Lord, may our lives:
express our love for you.

As we join our prayers with those of Mary,
may we learn from her responsive love:
Hail, Mary . . .

In silence, now,
we pour out to God our Father
any needs and burdens
known to us personally.

Silence

Celebrant
Heavenly Father,
trusting in your amazing love,
we ask you to accept these prayers.
Through Christ our Lord.
Amen.

THIRTY-SECOND SUNDAY OF THE YEAR

Life after death is not wishful thinking but a definite reality.

Celebrant
Let us pray to the great God of heaven
who stands among us now.

Reader
We pray that we, the earthly part of the Church,
may always reflect
the living presence of Christ among us,
in our liturgy and in our daily living.

Silence

You are our God:
living for ever and ever.

We pray for guidance in our world
as we work out policies and target needs,
and misunderstand one another's cultures
and get carried away with excesses
and the taste of power.

Silence

You are our God:
living for ever and ever.

We pray that our waking, working, eating,
relaxing and sleeping
may become a pattern coloured and lit by God's love;
may our homes reflect it,
our places of work be energised by it,
and our relationships glow with it.

Silence

You are our God:
living for ever and ever.

To those who are losing heart
we pray that the Lord may give
his heavenly encouragement and patience;
to the young and vulnerable
give his heavenly protection;
to the ill and the damaged
give his heavenly healing and inner peace,
as he touches our lives.

Silence

You are our God:
living for ever and ever.

Knowing that physical death
is not the end of life,
but the beginning of a new dimension,
we recall our loved ones who have died
and commend them to God's eternal keeping.

Silence

You are our God:
living for ever and ever.

We pray now with Mary,
Mother of our risen Lord:
Hail, Mary . . .

God our Father loves us as his children;
together in silence,
we name our personal prayer burdens.

Silence

Celebrant
All-powerful God, accept these prayers,
through Christ our Lord.
Amen.

THIRTY-THIRD SUNDAY OF THE YEAR

There will be dark and dangerous times
as the end approaches, but by standing firm
through it all we will gain life.

Celebrant
The Lord is always ready to listen;
let us pray to him now.

Reader
We pray particularly for those
whose faith is being battered
and those who no longer pray;
we pray that our faith
may be deepened and strengthened.

Silence

Lord, keep us faithful:
firm to the end.

We pray for those whose responsibility it is
to manage the world's economy,
and for those who have difficult
ethical decisions to make;
we pray for wisdom and courage to do what is right.

Silence

Lord, keep us faithful:
firm to the end.

We pray for the world our children will inherit
and ask blessings on all parents
and the responsibilities they face;
we ask for understanding, maturity,
and the gift of laughter.

Silence

Lord, keep us faithful:
firm to the end.

We pray for the victims of disasters,
famines, earthquakes and plagues;
for all who are crying
and those who have no tears left.
We pray for comfort, renewed strength,
and available friends.

Silence

Lord, keep us faithful:
firm to the end.

We pray for those who are nearing death
and those who have died;
especially we pray for those
who have died suddenly and unprepared.
We pray for mercy and forgiveness.

Silence

Lord, keep us faithful:
firm to the end.

We pray with Mary,
who followed her Son even to Calvary:
Hail, Mary . . .

In silence now,
we make our private petitions to God,
who knows what is in our hearts.

Silence

Celebrant
God our Father,
trusting in your constant care and protection,
we bring you these prayers.
Through Christ our Lord.
Amen.

CHRIST THE KING

*This Jesus, dying by crucifixion between criminals,
is the anointed King of all creation in whom all things are reconciled.*

Celebrant
Through Jesus, our King, let us pray to God the Father.

Reader
As we celebrate Jesus, the head of the Church body,
we pray for all the members
with their various gifts and ministries;
we pray that even our weaknesses
can be used for the glory of God
and for the good of the world.

Silence

Christ is the image:
of the invisible God we worship.

May all monarchs and heads of state
be led in ways of truth and righteousness,
and recognise with humility
that they are called to serve.
We pray for all shepherds,
rescue teams and trouble-shooters;
for all who work to recover the lost.

Silence

Christ is the image:
of the invisible God we worship.

May we reach out to one another
with greater love and better understanding;
we pray for our homes, our relatives,
our neighbours and our friends,
particularly those who do not yet realise
the extent of God's love for them.

Silence

Christ is the image:
of the invisible God we worship.

May those who have been scattered
far from their homes and loved ones
be enabled to live again in peace and happiness;
may the bitter and resentful find hope again
and the confused find new direction.

Silence

Christ is the image:
of the invisible God we worship.

May the dying know the closeness of God,
and those who mourn their loved ones
know for certain that God's kingdom
stretches across both sides of death.

Silence

Christ is the image:
of the invisible God we worship.

We pray with Mary,
Mother of Christ the King:
Hail, Mary . . .

In the warmth of God's love,
we pray in silence now
for our own particular concerns.

Silence

Celebrant
God our Father,
we ask you to accept our prayers,
through Christ our Lord.
Amen.

MARY, MOTHER OF GOD
1 JANUARY

Jesus Christ, the Son of God, is born of a woman.

Celebrant
Let us still our bodies and souls
as we gather to pray to the God
who made us and loves us.

Reader
As the Church we are the Body of Christ;
we give thanks for Mary's mothering
which we share with Jesus,
and pray that her love and faithfulness
will inspire in us a spirit of willing co-operation.

Silence

Your will, Lord:
be done in us.

Out of love for the world
God sent his Son into the world;
we pray for all who live in the darkness of sin,
for the places where evil and corruption flourish,
where the problems and troubles
seem almost too entrenched to be solved.
We pray for hearts to be healed of hatred
and hope to be rekindled.

Silence

Your will, Lord:
be done in us.

As we remember with gratitude
Mary's mothering in the home at Nazareth,
we pray for our own homes and families,
for all expectant mothers,
those giving birth and the children being born,
that they may be surrounded and upheld
with love and affection.

Silence

Your will, Lord:
be done in us.

As we call to mind those we know
who are in trouble, need or sorrow,
we pray for comfort and healing,
refreshment and encouragement.

Silence

Your will, Lord:
be done in us.

We give thanks that through the cross
death no longer has the victory;
we pray for those mothers who have died to this life
that they may know the fullness of joy in heaven.

Silence

Your will, Lord:
be done in us.

We pray with Mary,
our spiritual mother:
Hail, Mary . . .

Meeting our heavenly Father
in the stillness of silence,
let us whisper to him
our particular burdens of prayer.

Silence

Celebrant
Father, we bring these prayers
through Jesus Christ, our Saviour.
Amen.

THE PRESENTATION OF THE LORD (CANDLEMAS) – 2 FEBRUARY

*In accordance with Jewish tradition,
the Light of the World is presented as a first-born baby
in the temple at Jerusalem.*

Celebrant
As we gather in Christ's name,
let us bring to mind those
who particularly need our prayer support.

Reader
We remember those who teach the faith
throughout the Church and throughout the world.
May the Lord keep them close to his guiding,
and open the hearts of those they teach
to hear and receive his truth.

Silence

Show us your ways:
and help us to walk in them.

We remember those in positions
of authority and influence
in this country and in all societies,
that needs may be noticed and addressed,
good values upheld and all people respected.

Silence

Show us your ways:
and help us to walk in them.

We remember those who looked after us
when we were very young,
and those who have no one to love and care for them.
We remember all young families
and all the children in our parish,
that they may be introduced to the one true God
and live their lives in his company.

Silence

Show us your ways:
and help us to walk in them.

We remember the elderly faithful
and especially those who are housebound
and can no longer join us to worship in person.
We give thanks for their example
and pray for an increase of our love for one another
across the age groups.

Silence

Show us your ways:
and help us to walk in them.

We remember those who have finished
their lives on earth
and commit them to the Father's everlasting care
and protection.
We ask him to keep us faithful to the end of our life.

Silence

Show us your ways:
and help us to walk in them.

We offer our prayers with Mary
who took on the joys and sorrows
of mothering Jesus:
Hail, Mary . . .

In silence, let us bring to our God
the concerns of our own hearts,
knowing his love for us all.

Silence

Celebrant
Father, through the light of life
we are enabled to pray,
in the assurance of your faithfulness.
We offer our prayers
through Christ, the Light of the World.
Amen.

Saint John the Baptist – 24 June

John is born with a mission to prepare the way
for the Messiah by calling people to repentance.

Celebrant
Let us pray together in the presence of God.

Reader
Into every situation of doubt
and despondency among his followers
may the Father breathe his faithfulness.

Silence

Prepare us, O Lord:
to walk in your ways.

Into our strongholds of ambition
and defensiveness
may the Father breathe his humility.

Silence

Prepare us, O Lord:
to walk in your ways.

Into the prisons of guilt and revenge
may the Father breathe the grace of his forgiveness.

Silence

Prepare us, O Lord:
to walk in your ways.

Into the darkness of pain and fear
may the Father breathe his reassurance.

Silence

Prepare us, O Lord:
to walk in your ways.

Into our complacency
may the Father breathe his zeal.

Silence

Prepare us, O Lord:
to walk in your ways.

Into our homes and places of work
may the Father breathe his fellowship and love.

Silence

Prepare us, O Lord:
to walk in your ways.

Into the whole of his creation
may the father breathe his joy and peace.

Silence

Prepare us, O Lord:
to walk in your ways.

We make our prayer with Mary,
who rejoiced with her cousin Elizabeth
over the birth of John the Baptist:
Hail, Mary . . .

In silence, let us bring our private prayers
to the loving mercy of God.

Silence

Celebrant
Father, like John the Baptist,
may we courageously prepare the way
for the coming of the kingdom.
Through Christ, our Lord.
Amen.

SAINTS PETER AND PAUL – 29 JUNE

Through the dedication of the apostles Peter and Paul,
the Gospel of Jesus Christ spread and the Church was rapidly established.

Celebrant
Gathered as the Church of God,
let us pray.

Reader
As we celebrate the life and work of Peter and Paul,
we give thanks for our Church
and its faithfulness through the ages.
We ask the Lord to bless the Pope
and all leaders, pastors and teachers in the Church,
that they may be always open and attentive
to his guiding Spirit.

Silence

In all things, Father:
may your will be done.

As we recall the opposition and persecution
experienced by Peter and Paul,
we pray for all who are persecuted and threatened
for their faith today,
and for those working to discredit and crush
the influence of the Church.
We pray for the leaders of the nations
and those who advise and support them,
that they may seek what is right and good,
and bear in mind the needs of those they serve.

Silence

In all things, Father:
may your will be done.

We pray that in our daily prayers and conversations,
our daily work and service,
we may remain true to Christ's teaching
and love with his compassion,
whatever the cost.

Silence

In all things, Father:
may your will be done.

We pray for all who are imprisoned,
whether physically, emotionally or spiritually.
May the Lord free them to live in the freshness of his love
and the security of his faithfulness.

Silence

In all things, Father:
may your will be done.

As we recall with gratitude the willingness of Peter and Paul
to risk their lives in the Lord's service,
we pray for all who have died in faith
and thank the Lord for their love and commitment.
May he welcome them into his eternity;
may they know his peace and joy for ever.

Silence

In all things, Father:
may your will be done.

We join our prayers
with those of Mary our Mother:
Hail, Mary . . .

In the stillness of God's peace,
we bring our personal prayers
to our loving Father.

Silence

Celebrant
Father, accept these prayers
for the Church and for the world;
we pray that in all things
your kingdom may come.
Through Jesus Christ our Lord.
Amen.

THE TRANSFIGURATION OF THE LORD – 6 AUGUST

*Jesus is seen in all God's glory,
and as fulfilling the Law and the prophets.*

Celebrant
Let us quieten ourselves
in the presence of the living God,
as we pray.

Reader
The Father knows us better than we know ourselves,
and is well aware of the needs and pains
in his Church.
We lift them now to his healing love.

Silence

Father, we love you:
open our eyes to see your glory.

In our world there are decisions to be made,
countries to be governed and people to be honoured.
We lift them now to his grace and wisdom.

Silence

Father, we love you:
open our eyes to see your glory.

In our neighbourhood and in our homes
there are celebrations and tragedies,
times of hope, weariness and tenderness.
We lift them now to his parenting.

Silence

Father, we love you:
open our eyes to see your glory.

In our hospitals and clinics there are many in pain,
many who are fearful,
and many who have lost hope.
We lift them now to his comfort and protection.

Silence

Father, we love you:
open our eyes to see your glory.

As each day others die and enter his presence,
we ask his mercy
and commend them to his safekeeping.

Silence

Father, we love you:
open our eyes to see your glory.

We pray with Mary
who saw in her Son the glory of God:
Hail, Mary . . .

Let us be still and silent in God's presence
and pray in faith to our loving Father.

Silence

Celebrant
Father, as the disciples saw your glory
revealed in Jesus,
so may your glory be revealed in us.
Through Christ our Lord.
Amen.

THE ASSUMPTION – 15 AUGUST

The Almighty has done great things for me!

Celebrant
As children of our heavenly Father,
let us gather ourselves to pray.

Reader
On this feast of the Assumption,
we give thanks for the mothering love of Mary,
Mother of Christ and his Body, the Church.
We pray for each member of the Church of God,
both lay and ordained,
in their ministry to encourage one another
as loving servants to the needs of the world.

Silence

Lord of life:
may your kingdom come.

We pray for the world Christ died to save,
with its diversity of cultures and beliefs,
expectations and memories,
and its shared resources and human needs;
we pray for those who lead and govern,
for responsible stewardship
and wise decision-making.

Silence

Lord of life:
may your kingdom come.

We pray for our parents and our own families,
for all those we love and all who love us;
we pray for our friends and neighbours,
our colleagues, employers and employees;
we pray for those on either side of us now.

Silence

Lord of life:
may your kingdom come.

We pray for those who are in pain,
sorrow or distress,
that they may know God's presence
and receive his comfort and healing.

Silence

Lord of life:
may your kingdom come.

We pray for those who have died
and all who grieve for them;
we pray for those dying alone and unnoticed,
we pray for those dying unwanted and unborn.

Silence

Lord of life:
may your kingdom come.

We pray with Mary,
our Mother in heaven:
Hail, Mary . . .

In the silence of eternity,
let us bring to our loving Father
the concerns of our own hearts.

Silence

Celebrant
Father, with Mary we know
that you give us abundant blessing;
hear these prayers in mercy and love.
Through Christ our Lord.
Amen.

THE TRIUMPH OF THE HOLY CROSS
14 SEPTEMBER

*Through Christ's loving obedience,
even to death on a cross, he has opened up
the way for us to eternal life.*

Celebrant
In the knowledge of the extent of God's love for us,
let us pray.

Reader
We pray for all in the Church
whose journey through life is hard,
dangerous, exhausting or confused.

Silence

Lord of love:
you have won the victory.

We pray for those whose lives
are disrupted, oppressed or devastated
by war, famine or political unrest.

Silence

Lord of love:
you have won the victory.

We pray for our families, friends and neighbours;
all who cause us concern
and all in need of peace.

Silence

Lord of love:
you have won the victory.

We pray for those whose lives
are filled with pain, resentment or hatred;
for all who are trapped in addiction or despair.

Silence

Lord of love:
you have won the victory.

We pray for those who have died
and for those who miss them;
we thank the Lord for saving us through the cross
so that we can hope to share the glory of heaven.

Silence

Lord of love:
you have won the victory.

We join our prayers with those of Mary,
who witnessed the tragedy
and the triumph of the cross:
Hail, Mary . . .

As we kneel at the foot of the cross,
trusting in its power to save,
let us bring to the Lord our own prayers.

Silence

Celebrant
Father, you gave us the gift of your Son;
accept these prayers and transform our lives.
Through Christ our Lord.
Amen.

ALL SAINTS – 1 NOVEMBER

Lives that have shone with God's love on earth
are filled with joy as they see their Lord face to face.

Celebrant
Knowing our dependence on God in all things,
let us pray to him now.

Reader
As we celebrate the lives of those Church members
who have shone with the brightness of love,
we ask that the Lord may refresh our commitment
and conscious awareness of our need for him
in this parish and as individual Christians.

Silence

Just as I am:
I come.

May the kingdom of love and peace
be established in this world and grow.
We pray for both the influential and the ignored,
both the popular and the disliked,
both the ambitious and the vulnerable.
May the Lord teach us all his ways and his values.

Silence

Just as I am:
I come.

We call to mind our families and friends,
neighbours and colleagues,
giving thanks for all the loving care and forgiveness
the Lord has shown them,
and we ask him to shine his light
in all areas of hurt and misunderstanding.

Silence

Just as I am:
I come.

We bring to the God of healing
those whose lives are darkened by pain, fear or weariness.

May he come to our aid; help us to bear what must be carried,
and take from us all resentment and bitterness,
replacing it with the abundance of peace.

Silence

Just as I am:
I come.

We thank the eternal God for all the saints –
those recognised by the Church
and those known only to a few, and to him.
We rejoice that they live in heaven
with every tear wiped away.
May all who have died in the friendship of the Lord
know his mercy and lasting peace.

Silence

Just as I am:
I come.

May the gracious God take us as we are
and transform us by his life in us.
May he clear our lives of all that is not of him,
so that we let his goodness shine through the colours
of our personalities and gifts he has given us.

Silence

Just as I am:
I come.

We join our prayers with those of Mary
and all the saints:
Hail, Mary . . .

In a time of silence
and in the presence of all the saints in heaven,
let us pray for our particular concerns.

Silence

Celebrant
Father, as we celebrate the joy of those
whose wills are united with yours,
we commend to you our lives
and our hope of heaven,
through Christ our Lord.
Amen.

FEASTS OF THE DEDICATION OF A CHURCH

The church building symbolises the spiritual temple,
being built of the living stones of God's people.

Celebrant
Gathered as the Church of Christ in this place,
let us pray together in his name.

Reader
We give thanks for this church building
and the privilege of worshipping without fear.
We give thanks for all
who have prayed and ministered here,
and ask that the Lord will keep us attentive to his voice,
worshipping him in spirit and in truth.

Silence

Take us, Lord:
renew us and use us.

We pray for this area and its problems,
for all who live, work and raise their families here.
We give thanks for all that is good and hopeful,
and ask the Lord to bless and guide those in authority.

Silence

Take us, Lord:
renew us and use us.

May the homes we represent and all the homes of this parish
be filled with light and love,
warmth and welcome,
comfort and peace.

Silence

Take us, Lord:
renew us and use us.

May all who come to this place
in distress of body or soul
find here healing and refreshment,
and be touched with the beauty of God's holiness.

Silence

Take us, Lord:
renew us and use us.

We commend to the Father's love
all those who have worshipped here in the past,
both those we remember
and those known only to him.

Silence

Take us, Lord:
renew us and use us.

We make our prayers with Mary,
the Mother of the Church:
Hail, Mary . . .

In a time of silence, filled with God's peace,
we bring our personal prayers and petitions,
in the assurance of God's love.

Silence

Celebrant
Father, hear these prayers
which we offer as your people,
and build us as living stones
into a spiritual temple.
Through Christ our Lord.
Amen.